My Hallucinations

Journey beyond Universe

Vedha

BookLeaf Publishing

India | USA | UK

To my beloved daughter, Gauri Parvati,

*Your unwavering encouragement and vibrant
spirit inspire every word I write.*

*You are my muse, my greatest supporter and my
reminder*

that dreams flourish with love and belief.

*—**With all my love,***

Acknowledgements

The creation of My Hallucinations has been an unforgettable journey, made possible by the love, encouragement and unwavering support of my incredible family.

To my amazing daughter, your endless enthusiasm and belief in me have been my guiding light. You've been my biggest motivator, always ready to help with creative ideas, problem-solving and the tech challenges that came my way. Your passion and energy have made this journey truly special.

To my son, your quiet strength and calm presence have been just as essential. Whether offering thoughtful advice, helping in moments of doubt or simply being there with your support, you've been a steady source of comfort and encouragement.

To my husband, thank you for being my rock. Your belief in my work, your invaluable technical expertise and your constant encouragement have helped me push through every hurdle. You've been my partner in every sense of the word, and I am forever grateful.

Each of you has played a unique and irreplaceable role in bringing this book to life. From navigating technology and design to offering kind words and endless patience, this book is as much yours as it is mine. Thank you for being my family, my team and my inspiration.

With all my love and gratitude,

Preface

Poetry is the bridge between the heart and the universe – a tapestry of emotions, dreams and the mysteries that surround us. My Hallucinations is a collection of poems inspired by the boundless beauty of the cosmos, the infinite expanse of galaxies and the secrets of the universe that have always fuelled my imagination and creativity.

For as long as I can remember, I have been captivated by the stars above and the wonders they represent. These celestial mysteries have influenced not just my thoughts, but also the way I perceive life, love and the delicate dance between reality and dreams. Through this collection, I hope to capture the essence of those inspirations and share the vivid imagery and emotions they stir within me.

This book has been a long time in the making – a dream nurtured over countless nights of reflection and creativity. Finally, the time has come to give life to these verses and offer them to kindred spirits who seek wonder in the mysteries of life and the universe. It is my hope that My Hallucinations will transport you into realms both familiar and unknown, where the imagination roams freely and the universe whispers its secrets to those who listen.

With gratitude and wonder,

Facing the Abyss

A meeting with a void and myself
That deeply connects me with the cosmos.
It is not just a difficulty or an obstacle,
It is a mysterious force
That challenges the bound boundaries of my
existence,
A confrontation with nihilism.
It is an emotional whirlwind,
Where I wrestled with the demons of my mind
And sought refuge.
There is an enigmatic force at the edge of the
abyss,
Or is it the abyss,
An expression or even transcended?
It is not a metaphor or lack of purpose,
It is a journey which has isolated me
From conventions of time,
Detonating me from sanity.
When I gaze long into an abyss,
It looks back at me.
It is not a neutral space,
It is a mental breakdown of silence
Which challenges, tests and sometimes consumes.
Enduring a constant battle against my emotions,
It is a desperate yearning

To find beauty amidst chaos.
The shadow of me that I deny,
Internal struggles and mystical dreams–
It is a space of my transformation,
A mirror of unfathomable events
Which enables me to see through them.
My obsessive desire to explore my limits,
A space where the dark night of the soul
Proceeds to enlightenment–
The path of Nirvana.
My emotional turbulence is mirrored in the
cosmos.
It is not a place of redemption and learning,
But a brutal reminder
Of our insignificance in the cosmos.
Moments like surrealism
Draw inspiration from the abyss.
It is a space of unconscious symphony
Which captures both anguish
And spiritual elevation.
It is a place of pain and ruin,
But the truth.
A space where I am forced to challenge myself
To create meaning amid chaos,
Light in the darkness,
And to rebuild where everything seemed lost.
It is an illustration of my deranged mind.

Battle with Hallucination

I invite you into my space right away,
To discern if this is real or a fleeting dream.
You are my hallucination,
A sensation that intoxicates me.

In my vertigo, my dizziness, my drunken haze,
I whirl and dance like a spinning wheel.
You emerge as the source of my existence,
Yet my words are but nonsensical echoes.

A haunting image amidst serenity and joy,
Your silent look with my drooping eyes,
Reveals an unknown world of hallucination.

Shadows follow me into the dark side,
Where light is needless, we thrive in the abyss.
Fool me like I'm dreaming, through the invisible
light,
As colours and shades elude my grasp,
Leaving behind only shadows of hallucination.

Mistaken notions of divine feelings,
That inspire wonders for some–
Yet for others, mere thoughts pass by.

In a trance, without truly knowing,
My heart feels it, though reason escapes me.
Subconscious pictures dance wildly,
Clashing with consciousness on my window
panes.
Devils flirt with my struggling serenity,
Pinning me to nonexistent possibilities.

But I know this storm will pass,
I will gather myself and rise.
Through the chaos, I will prevail,
And win this battle with hallucination.

Our incomplete story

In the stillness of the night, I hear your name,
A whisper that dances through shadows, aflame.
When you were near, my woods bloomed with
light,
Now they stand silent, cloaked in twilight.

We were a promise, carved in letters of love,
Now just a memory, with scars to speak of.
Time tore apart the chapters we dreamed,
Our love, a story unfinished, it seems.

We reached so close, yet the voids remained,
An endless horizon where our love refrained.
The tides of time washed us away,
Yet your essence lingers, come what may.

Not every orbit circles the sun,
Even in absence, you're never undone.
You are my constant, my unbroken part,
A shadow etched deep within my heart.

I walk these streets we wandered as one,
Each step whispers of the joy we spun.
Corners hold echoes of our laughter's refrain,
Ghosts of a love that still remains.

My love is a puzzle, chaotic yet whole,
Passion and pain intertwined in my soul.
Your absence sharpens the depth of your mark,
Thoughts of you linger, igniting the dark.

The pages of us, faded and torn,
Await another life where love is reborn.
Where missing lines find their rightful place,
And time no longer leaves its trace.

Until then, I hold you close in my mind,
A love unending, a bond undefined.
Though our tale is unfinished, untold,
You remain my treasure, my heart's pure gold.

Dance of Two Souls

When two souls entwine, a silent symphony
begins,
A yearning so profound, it transcends touch and
time.
Their presence is a melody–
Felt in the clasp of a hand, the cadence of a voice,
Or the fleeting curve of a smile that lingers like
twilight.

Not all believe in soulmates, but I do–
A faith in the one crafted to complete another's
essence.
He is the quiet in your storm, the shield in your
battle,
The unwavering lighthouse through the fog of
sorrow.
He knows your unspoken thoughts before they
take shape,
A mirror reflecting your truest self.

Together, you sculpt each other with tender
hands,
Chiselling imperfections to fit like ancient puzzle
pieces.
This is how soulmates are forged–

Not in fire, but in the soft glow of understanding,
In the sanctuary of unspoken belief.

A soulmate sees you before the world does,
Holds your heart as if it were a fragile star.
They breathe life into your dreams,
And you, in their presence, rise to meet your
better self.

Love becomes an elixir, intoxicating and infinite,
A rhythm neither calendar nor clock can measure.
Time and distance dissolve in their embrace,
For their essence is timeless, their bond eternal.

With them, you are more yourself than ever
before,
Unmasked, vulnerable, yet invincible.
Their touch reaches the hidden chambers of your
soul,
Where secrets reside, whispered only to them.

Every smile becomes a bridge to a past you've
never known,
Every whisper, an echo of lifetimes long gone.
It feels as though you have loved them
In some distant existence, beneath another sky,
In a place untouched by the hands of time.

It is the language of two souls, ancient and sacred,
A connection so profound, it defies words—
A celestial thread woven through the universe,
Binding hearts that were always meant to be one.

The Dark Side

On the edge of my consciousness, where whispers
dwell,
Deep within the labyrinth of my mind,
Lurks a shadow – nameless, formless, eternal.
It lingers behind my eyes, cloaked in darkness,
A silent companion to my every breath.

Is it my strength, a fortress unseen?
Or my weakness, a whisper of defeat?
A tempest of adrenaline coursing through veins,
Or the quiet echo of lingering sorrow?
This shadow evades definition,
A shapeshifter, a riddle unspoken.

If I could name it, would it vanish like mist?
Yet it plays its games, a dance of hide and seek.
At times, it clasps my hand,
Pulling me into sunlight's warm embrace,
Painting my world with vivid hues,
Whispering, 'You are invincible'.

Other times, it unravels me,
A burst of crimson like a fallen star,
Collapsing into the void of its making.
This darkness – enemy or ally?

A paradox, light's eternal counterpart,
Two faces of a single coin, entwined in their
design.

With time, I learned to stop running.
To deny it was to give it power,
To fight it was to splinter myself.
So I opened my arms to its shadowy form,
Embraced its presence as a friend,
A quiet peace settling where chaos once reigned.

Redemption lies not in erasure,
But in the delicate balance of duality,
For this shadow is me, as much as the light.
It walks with me through every crest and trough,
Its hand in mine, steadying my steps.

Together, we are whole.
For only when I embrace the dark,
Do I truly see the brilliance of the light.

Solitude

Loneliness slips in like a cunning thief,
Plundering warmth, planting seeds of grief.
In the stillness, I bear its weight,
An abyss within I cannot sate.

The world drifts distant, blurred, estranged,
A muted whisper, cold and unchanged.
Eyes lost in the boundless void,
Where shadows of silence are deployed.

No voices, no laughter, no tender embrace,
Just a drifting soul in an empty space.
It ambushes me, unbidden, sly,
A tempest beneath a quiet sky.

Lurking in corners, poised to attack,
A spectre that whispers of what I lack.
It grips my heart with piercing claws,
A silent war without applause.

In the hush of hours when the world is still,
It seeps through cracks, bending my will.
Tears trace paths, sorrow remains,
A captive soul bound by its chains.

Yet even in darkness, hope softly glows,
A fragile ember that steadily grows.
Through shadows deep, I'll find my way,
And banish the night with the dawn's first ray.

Nature's Symphony

It's a rainy morning; the earth feels new,
The sky draped in a silken, misty hue.
I wander forth, through nature's embrace,
A world alive, a tranquil place.

The landscape gleams, a vivid spread,
Colours bloom where the raindrops tread.
A painter's dream, a poet's muse,
In drizzled tones, the heart renews.

The melody of rain, a soothing song,
A lullaby where the soul belongs.
Raindrops kiss the earth with grace,
Clouds roll softly, their rhythms trace.

The foggy peaks stand proud, serene,
Majestic sentinels in nature's scene.
Childlike wonder awakens in me,
Lost in this purest revelry.

She, like a siren, enchants the eye,
A lustrous beauty beneath the sky.
Her tender touch, her glittering guise,
A radiant wonder that never lies.

I close my eyes, let her essence flow,
Her love, a balm, her spirit aglow.
Refreshed, reborn, I breathe her air,
A gift of joy beyond compare.

With every step, her whispers call,
A reminder: I am part of it all.
Nature's symphony, vibrant and true,
Awakens the soul, paints life anew.

The Shadow Within

Depression creeps, a thief of grace,
Stealing light from the brightest place.
Uninvited, it storms through my door,
Leaving my spirit battered and sore.

No courtesy, no gentle tread,
It plants chaos inside my head.
A hurricane raging, relentless and wild,
Turning my mind into a lost, broken child.

It draws me deep into its lair,
Pitch-black cold, an empty stare.
Rules unspoken, cruel games it plays,
Binding my thoughts in a shrouded haze.

Not a friend, nor a guiding muse,
Just a tormentor with lies it infuses.
'You're worthless, ugly,' it cruelly proclaims,
Calling out flaws, igniting shame.

Yet, beneath its taunts, a mirror it shows,
Bare truths unfiltered, the pain it sows.
Stripping illusions, my soul laid bare,
A silent battle, a cross to bear.

Days turn to nights; the cycle persists,
Draining my will, till nothing exists.
I curl in my cocoon, a fragile retreat,
Hoping for solace, the storm to defeat.

But within me burns a steadfast flame,
A whispering voice that calls my name.
'I've conquered battles, I've weathered the fight,
This shadow won't steal my inner light'.

I rise, though trembling, I meet my eyes,
In the mirror where my reflection lies.
'You are more than this moment', I softly say,
'A masterpiece still finding its way'.

Each step I take, I reclaim my space,
Piece by piece, I embrace my grace.
Depression's shadow may linger near,
But it cannot conquer what I hold dear.

For I am the phoenix, born anew,
A precious soul breaking through.
This is not the end; my story's begun,
And I will shine brighter than the sun.

Healing

A quiet strength buried deep within,
A realm you once believed beyond reach.
Healing is no sudden miracle;
It's a gradual ascent – a journey of perseverance.

One step at a time, day by day,
You grow resilient, mind and spirit entwined.
Each dawn brings a better version of you.
Heal at your rhythm; embrace your pace.
Rise when you are ready–
Move forward when the time feels right.

It begins with the soul's awakening,
Stirred by the weight of pain.
When anguish reaches its zenith,
Do not return to what broke you.
Instead, sit with the ache, trace its roots.
Uncover the source, sever its lifeline.
Wrap the wounds in tender care,
And let the lingering sorrow fade in time.
Break, if you must, into shards,
Only to rebuild yourself,
Stronger, steadier, whole once more.

On the path of recovery,

You'll find yourself transformed:
Judging less, observing more,
Responding with grace, not reacting in haste.
Nurturing self-love over self-doubt.
Setting boundaries over bending to sentiment.
Choosing inner peace over external turmoil,
Clarity over confusion,
Being overdoing,
Faith over fear.

Heal not for yourself alone,
For unhealed souls scatter pain like seeds.
As you mend, you'll feel reborn:
No longer tolerating but calmly ignoring.
No longer silenced but true to your essence.
What once incited battles within,
Now fades into irrelevance.

When you heal, you unveil your worth–
An untouchable brilliance, undimmed by past
trials.
You reserve your energy for what uplifts,
For what deserves your light.
You are healed, whole,
And free to flourish once more.

The Becoming

For years, you clung to a facade, a brittle illusion–
Believing you knew yourself, or pretending to.
You wore masks forged by expectations,
Shaped yourself to fit into moulds
That were never crafted for your soul.

Shrouded in a cloak of pretence,
You lost the essence of who you were.

The unravelling was neither swift nor gentle.
It was a brutal reckoning,
Peeling back layers of identity–
Raw, excruciating, unrelenting.
The scaffolding of years, dismantled with ferocity,
People, places, habits – anchors turned into
chains.
Familiar comforts tightened their grip
Even as you yearned to break free.

Letting go felt like severing limbs.
The parts you once cherished,
Now foreign and unrecognisable,
Slipped through your grasp like sand.
It was dread incarnate,
A slow trudge through the mire.

Every realisation cut like jagged glass,
Discordant and cruel,
Stripping harmony from your world.

Change does not arrive with fireworks;
It crawls, inch by painful inch.
Progress felt like small triumphs
Shadowed by the mourning of who you used to
be.
Each shed layer revealed new frequencies–
Unfamiliar, awkward, alien.

But within the dissonance, there was a whisper:
You are nearing the truth.
Acceptance rose, unbidden yet welcome,
A tranquil tide stilling the stormy seas.

The harder you resisted, the more savage the
current.
Surrender was the only way forward.
Flow with it, let it carry you,
Trust the rhythm of transformation.
In yielding, you found strength.

The journey is never uniform.
For each soul, it carves a unique path,
Marked by anguish and revelation.
These moments of pain – brutal yet necessary–

Are the architects of wisdom,
Teaching the grace of surrender.

Now, as you look back, the truth gleams:
You were never losing yourself.
You were unearthing the core,
Not broken, but remade.
Slowly, painfully,
Utterly whole.

Always and Forever

A quiet beauty, serene yet profound,
You draw me in, like gravity unbound.
Every glance – a spark, a gentle trance,
The first step in our eternal dance.
You've turned my life into a symphony,
A melody where I finally see
That with you, I've found where I'm meant to be.

This love runs deeper than oceans can claim,
A boundless force, untamed, unframed.
In the cadence of your voice, a love so clear,
It pulls me closer, erases all fear.
In your arms, the world finds its light,
A haven, a shield, my endless night.
You've shown me love in its truest art,
A story etched in the depths of my heart.

Your laughter – an echo, a timeless refrain,
A melody that sweetens even the rain.
Your love is the rhythm my soul beats to,
Deeper than seas, boundless and true.
You changed my world, like dawn's first light,
You are my peace, my home, my flight.

I never knew love could feel this vast,
A radiant glow, outshining the past.
I'll love you through shadows, tides and miles,
Through every storm, with steadfast smiles.
Each touch is the prologue, a spark divine,
Of a tale written in your hand and mine.

With you, I've unearthed what I was seeking,
A love so profound, my soul is singing.
You've turned my darkness into starlit skies,
A love so pure, no room for disguise.
Forever is ours, an endless delight,
With you, my love, the world feels right.

Whispers in the dark

In the hush of midnight's tender grace,
I feel your breath, though not a trace.
Your love, a beacon guiding me through,
A dream, a phantom, yet achingly true.

Whispers murmur, soft and low,
Calling your name where shadows grow.
The night enfolds us, a velvet shroud,
Moonlight paints you, pale and proud.

Time surrenders, the world takes flight,
No fears to haunt, no lurking fright.
This darkness holds a truth so stark–
Our love, unspoken, whispers in the dark.

Silence blooms where hearts collide,
No need to flee, no place to hide.
Your whispers weave through the starlit skies,
A song eternal that never dies.

Beneath the heavens' shimmering glow,
I dance in the dream where our love flows.
Each beat of my heart, a spark divine,
An echo of you, a lifeline.

Is this a dream, or some fleeting trace,
Of love imagined in this quiet space?
Night begins, yet never ends,
As love transcends, the soul ascends.

Complete, I linger in this fleeting spark,
Lost in your whispers, eternal, in the dark.

The Love We Wrote Together

You haunt my thoughts, a vivid dream,
A love that pulses, fierce, supreme.
When you stepped into my weary life,
Eternity stirred, and time took flight.

It began as an ember, a quiet spark,
Two untamed souls in a boundless arc.
We etched our dreams on time's vast slate,
Each stroke a vow, defying fate.

Every page, each verse we bled,
Ink of devotion, deeply fed.
Your hand in mine, our hearts aligned,
A symphony rare, profoundly designed.

This love we've forged, unyielding, true,
A saga eternal – me and you.
Through tempests wild and skies set ablaze,
Our bond endures, through nights and days.

Our story roars, untamed, profound,
A melody sung where hearts resound.
This is the love we wrote together,

A legend to echo forever and ever.

Serenity

In the hum of life, I find my calm,
A quiet pulse, a soothing balm.
Not in rivers, nor in blooming fields,
But within, where silence yields.

The chaos fades, the noise subsides,
Like restless waves on ebbing tides.
I close my eyes and draw a breath,
A moment stolen from life's depth.

Tranquillity whispers, soft and pure,
A fleeting peace, yet so secure.
No need for landscapes, painted skies–
Just the stillness behind closed eyes.

Thoughts once wild, now gently flow,
Like softened streams where breezes go.
The mind unwinds, the soul aligns,
In this sanctuary undefined.

Serenity blooms, a quiet art,
A haven built within the heart.
Amid the rush, I pause and stay–
A sacred stillness, my hideaway.

Eternal Bliss

The first cry, the first gaze–
Her face, serene as a moonlit night,
A quiet peace swept through me.
The pain dissolved,
Replaced by the magic of her smile.

Once a part of me,
Now the world holds her as its own.
Cradling her,
It felt as if time had gifted me a treasure,
A diamond to nurture, a wonder to cherish.

Words fall short for what I feel–
A boundless joy, a tranquil heaven,
A love that soothes the chaos of life.
In her, I've found my sanctuary,
My calm, my endless light.

She is my guiding star,
Illuminating life's untamed roads.
My daughter, my eternal bliss.

Lunatic

In the abyss of silence, I seek bliss,
A fleeting hour where shadows hiss.
My soul, captive in night's dark clasp,
Clings to whispers of a love long past.

Through a cracked window, light tries to seep,
Infatuations stir from their restless sleep.
How I ache to revive that fervent flame,
Eyes meeting eyes, trembling, untamed.

The grey canvas hums with fractured dreams,
Each shard a tempest, a muffled scream.
My heart, a chalice of poisoned devotion,
Drenched in the ache of wild emotion.

Lost in the haze of a midnight sky,
A lunatic's lament, untamed, awry.
Delusions ripple, fierce and wild,
A storm within – a love exiled.

What Love Left Behind

I thought love was celestial, timeless, pure,
A sacred hymn, an eternal allure.
I nurtured it like a fragile flame,
Only to wonder – was it ever the same?

I loved you with an unyielding heart,
Each fleeting moment, a masterpiece of art.
Yet, in the shadows, the whispers grew thin,
And I stood bewildered – where did we begin?

Your gaze, once luminous, now feels veiled,
A language once fluent, now fractured, derailed.
I reach into the chasm where we stood entwined,
But all I grasp is the echo of time.

Love, a hallowed altar, I knelt in devotion,
Only to find it a fleeting illusion.
It poured its joy, then carved its sting,
A cruel symphony that loss can bring.

Yet amidst the wreckage, I find faint grace,
The ghost of your laughter, your fleeting embrace.
A bittersweet relic I dare not release,
A fragment of you, my paradox of peace.

Love is a tempest, both fierce and sublime,
A fleeting mirage, a thief of time.
It grants us wings, then leaves us torn,
A sanctuary lost, a soul reborn.

Though I no longer know your way,
I hold the fragments of our yesterday.
A love that taught me to endure,
Both haunting and divine, forever unsure.

The Power of Tears

A storm within, a shattered core,
Pain pounding louder than ever before.
Thunder in my heart, my spirit undone,
A battle I lost, retreating, alone.

I sought refuge in melody's embrace,
Lyrics and rhythms, a fleeting trace.
Yet nothing could mend the fractured seams,
No music could soothe my broken dreams.

Then a tear fell, soft and unspoken,
A silent stream for a soul left broken.
And as it flowed, a surge so profound,
Strength arose where despair had drowned.

Tears became whispers, gentle and true,
Healing wounds as they carved paths anew.
They spoke of courage, of trials faced,
Of resilience found, of sorrows erased.

Now I cherish the rivers that flow,
For in their depth, strength does grow.
A testament to the storms endured,
Tears, my balm, my soul assured.

Rage of the Void

A savage storm consumed my core,
Cold and cruel, I craved no more.
Heartless fury, wild and raw,
No mercy bound by love or law.

The night possessed my fractured mind,
Ruthless, reckless, unrefined.
No face could calm, no voice could tame,
A beast unleashed, unbound by shame.

Yet morning broke, with golden breath,
And pulled me back from shadowed death.
There you stood, your steadfast gaze,
Dispelling madness, softening haze.

The tempest stilled, its wrath erased,
In love's firm hold, my soul embraced.

Silent Confession

I have loved you in whispers, in unspoken dreams,
A melody unheard, flowing through quiet
streams.
You move like poetry, a verse in the air,
Yet I stand in silence, too lost to declare.

They say you love like seasons change,
A fleeting breeze, wild and strange.
But when you're near, my world takes flight,
A heart unchained, set alight.

I try to speak, yet words betray,
A trembling voice drifts away.

Unspoken Words

You say it all without a sound,
A steady presence, strong and profound.
No need for words, no grand display,
Yet in your silence, you light my way.

The curve of your smile, the calm in your eyes,
Speak of promises, steady and wise.
A touch so firm, a glance so true,
Says, I am here – for all of you.

Through storms you stand, quiet but near,
Shielding us softly from struggle and fear.
You carry the weight, yet never complain,
Giving your all through joy and pain.

No whispered vows, no need to declare,
Your love is felt, always there.
For the loudest truths, the deepest care,
Are spoken best in the quiet air.

Echoes of You

I still feel you in the quiet air,
Fragments of moments we used to share.
Your words once held me, calm and true,
Now they linger, shadows of you.

The hours we spent, the worlds we built,
Fade like whispers, leaving me spilt.
You were my storm's still, gentle eye,
Now you're the ache I can't deny.

Though you're gone, the void remains,
A hollow tune in love's refrain.
I miss the you that felt so near,
And the me that lived when you were here.

Cleansed by the Storm

Upon the cliffs, she sits, burdened and bare,
Waves roar below; their thunder fills the air.
Dark waters churn, restless and wild,
Echoing the storm within the exiled.

Clouds gather, heavy, a shroud of despair,
Raindrops fall like shards, slicing the air.
Each droplet pierces, sharp and cold,
Yet softens her grief, her story untold.

The wind whispers, caressing her face,
A tender balm, a fleeting embrace.
The rain flows gently, washing her clean,
Healing the hurt, unseen and serene.

Nature's tempest becomes her reprieve,
Its fierce embrace, a reason to believe.
Amid the chaos, her spirit takes flight,
Soothed by the storm, bathed in its light.

Ebb and Flow

The cruellest part is not the fall,
But knowing it's coming–
A slow descent into the abyss,
Where shadows whisper, demons linger,
And the darkness becomes my captor.

I scream for help, a muted cry,
Yet no rescue comes before the plunge.
I brace for sorrow's weight,
For the bitter embrace of despair.
I know I will climb again–
Scraping, clawing, fighting–
But the pit is deep, the struggle endless.

And when I rise, oh, how I rise!
Energy surges like an untamed storm,
A flood of brilliance, boundless and bright.
I become more than mortal–
A cosmic force, a divine spark,
Speaking languages I've never known,
Dancing on the edge of the infinite.

But at the summit, the flame consumes.
A pill, a voice of reason, pulls me down.
Sedated, tethered, I drift back to calm–

To normalcy, to balance, to me.

Then, as surely as the sun sets,
The tide shifts, and I fall again.
This is my journey–
A pendulum of pain and brilliance,
Of crashing lows and soaring highs.

Yet I manage; I endure.
Thanks to hands that steady me–
Me, myself within,
My husband, my family, my doctor's care.
They are my anchors in the storm,
My light when all else fades.

For I am bipolar, a warrior of the mind,
Living a life of cycles, of tides within.
And though the battle is unending,
I survive, I thrive, I live.

The Midnight Vigil

Eyes wide, heavy with exhaustion,
A timid soul tangled in restlessness,
Craving sleep's tender embrace–
Yet the clock ticks past tomorrow,
And slumber evades my grasp.

No tormenting thoughts, no aching fears,
No shadow of sorrow pressing near.
Still, the night stretches, vast and unyielding,
An unseen energy stirs within,
Keeping my weary spirit alight.

Stars blink in their cosmic rhythm,
Mocking my sleepless rebellion.
Nature whispers its lullabies,
But my mind, a maze of fragile threads,
Wanders lost in its labyrinth.

The doctor's voice lingers, a distant echo:
'Fight back. Seek rest. Heal.'
Yet here I lie, caught in insomnia's snare,
A fragile rebellion against my own design,
Waiting for morning to break the spell.

The Masks I Wear

I am a social being,
Bound to the world's unspoken rules.
But the tides within me – bipolar, unrelenting–
Make mingling a battlefield.
I have my haven, my chosen few,
Yet life pulls me into unfamiliar crowds,
Where I must play the part.

So I wear a mask.
A smile, painted with precision,
Hiding the chaos beneath.
My face betrays me at times,
But I cannot let the pain escape.
No restlessness, no pride, no vulnerability–
Only the facade they expect to see.

In a room of chatter and cheer,
I am both present and apart.
I talk, or I shrink to the shadows,
Avoiding words that pierce too deep.
The mask is heavy,
But I carry it still,
Not to deceive, but to survive.

They don't see the struggle–

The silent battles, the storms within.
To them, I am whole, perfect, complete.
And perhaps, in a way, I am blessed.
For I have my anchors:
My radiant daughter,
My steadfast son,
And the protector of my life, my husband–
The one who sees me, truly sees me,
And embraces all that I am.

With them, I am unmasked,
Raw, real and free.
They hold me through the highs and lows,
Through the fractures and the mending.
Their love is my sanctuary,
Their acceptance, my strength.

But out there, in the world's glare,
I wear my many masks.
Not to pretend, but to protect,
To navigate this maze of social order.
I am the woman of a thousand faces,
And beneath each lies the truth–
A soul fighting, surviving,
And moving forward,
One masked step at a time.

Unmasked

Bare, brittle, shadows collide,
Walls shattered, nowhere to hide.
Laughter cuts, my flaws laid bare,
Naked truth, a raw despair.

Questions spiral, answers stray,
Is this me, or did I betray?
Exposed, I linger in the ache,
A soul unguarded, bound to break.

Yet in the shards, a faint embrace,
The weight of truth, a fragile grace.
Perhaps in ruin, I'll find my ground,
In naked light, I am unbound.

Lucid Whispers

Eyes closed, I drift, not far but deep,
Dreams unfurl where shadows seep.
A realm so vivid, yet undefined,
A world I walk with an awakened mind.

Is it life lived in a fleeting glow,
A dimension where lost realities grow?
Time bends, it twists, it fades away,
An entire life in the span of a stay.

Waking, I wonder – was it truly mine?
A glimpse of the infinite, outside of time.
Dreams are whispers of worlds unseen,
A lucid voyage through what might have been.

The Path of Seeking

When consciousness unfurls its wings,
Unbound by time, unfazed by space,
It grazes the edge of dreams with fleeting touch,
While sanity drifts, untethered,
A quiet rebellion against earthly cadence.
I wander on broken grains of sand–
Stranded, a migrant soul adrift,
Lost at sea, engulfed by the ache of knowing too
little,
And yearning for the unseen.

Beyond the veils of what eyes perceive,
Dimensions stretch, infinite and unknowable.
Not a universe, but multiverses pulsate,
Each a ripple in the cosmic void.
Is it the consciousness I chase,
The beginning of all that is – or nothingness
itself?
Far beyond the galaxies' celestial embrace,
Lies a truth I seek, elusive, eternal,
A whisper hidden in the folds of space-time.

I devour ancient texts,
Echoes of civilisations long erased by shifting
sands.

I listen to the wise,
Those who tread this path of yearning before me.
Some name it spirituality,
But I call it seeking–
A restless pursuit of a truth
That eludes both language and form.

This land, this sacred cradle of seekers,
Bears the weight of timeless wisdom.
Sanatan Dharma flows through its veins,
Guiding wanderers to the infinite.
Our sages whispered of cosmic layers,
Worlds within worlds,
Dimensions unmeasured,
Where creation began in the hum of nothingness,
Where silence birthed the first vibration.

I believe Earth is but a fragment,
A single thread in an endless loom.
Galaxies themselves are but specks,
And existence – merely an echo of a greater song.
I reach for the ungraspable,
Not to find, but to journey.

Truth is not my destination,
For it already exists within and without.
But the how – the passage, the unfolding,
The unravelling of this enigma–

That is the flame I follow.
I tread an unmarked path,
Footsteps fading in the sand behind me,
A traveller of time,
A seeker of the infinite unknown.

Perhaps I will never reach the end,
Perhaps the journey itself is the answer.
But I will wander still,
With a heart set ablaze by curiosity,
A mind unchained by boundaries,
And a soul that dances
In the rhythm of seeking.

The Storm Within

In stillness, I sat, seeking destiny's thread,
When a storm awakened, fierce and widespread.
Chains of illusion shattered apart,
A thousand stars ignited my heart.

Winds from the past, relentless, roared,
Pulling me through truths unexplored.
Fragments of self, scattered and spun,
A thousand me's orbiting a single sun.

The life I knew, a dream now blurred,
Echoes of choices, chances deferred.
Weightless I drifted through realms untold,
Drawn by a force both tender and bold.

A light, eternal, pierced through space,
Neither joy nor pain – just boundless grace.
It pulled me close, yet kept me free,
A glimpse of the infinite mystery.

As the storm stilled, my breath aligned,
The cosmos faded, and I returned to my mind.
Yet a spark remained, a quiet flame,
The storm had whispered the truth's name.

Was it divine? A cosmic sign?
A call to realms where truths entwine.
The journey began with that storm inside,
A cosmic pull towards the infinite tide.

Eclipsing Eternity

Through galaxies woven in threads of light,
I drift – a traveller of infinite night.
Stars whisper secrets in tongues unknown,
Their echoes carved in time-worn stone.

A garden of dreams unfolds in space,
Petals of longing, woven with grace.
Rivers of ambition, ceaseless, untamed,
Yet thirsting for joy that remains unnamed.

I walk through forests where shadows dance,
Where greed and chaos twirl in trance.
Mountains rise with wisdom untold,
Their peaks are silent, yet fierce and bold.

The horizon glows in hues of fire,
A burning sun of endless desire.
Winter weeps in ivory shrouds,
While summer hums in golden clouds.

Love arrives like a fleeting breeze,
Soft as whispers between the trees.
Yet hate lurks in tempest's call,
Breaking, bending, consuming all.

Faces pass like spectral light,
Some to heal, some to fight.
A hand to guide, a voice to break,
A soul to mend, a heart to take.

Through valleys of sorrow, I lose my way,
Hope flickers, a dying ray.
Yet from the wreckage, dawn unfurls,
A phoenix born of shattered worlds.

I chased illusions, silver and gold,
Built my kingdoms, watched them fold.
The more I sought, the less I found,
In fleeting echoes, I was bound.

But then – like fire in a breathless void,
A voice within, clear yet devoid.
'Unravel the veil, seek beyond sight,
The truth you long for is not in the light.'

No weight of riches, no kingdom's throne,
No love nor loss I truly own.
I dissolve, I rise, I break, I mend,
The self was never mine to defend.

And at the end – if end there be,
I'll melt into eternity.
Not lost, nor found, but free to roam,
A spark returned to light's own home.

9 789369 543304